Columbus Day

by Vicki Liestman
illustrations by Rick Hanson

Carolrhoda Books · Minneapolis, Minnesota

For Tim
  —V.L.

To Jeanne, Meggan, Nolan, and Eric
                    —R.H.

Special thanks to Dr. Jean O'Brien,
Native American History, University
of Minnesota, for her assistance with
this book.

This edition of this book is available in two bindings:
Library binding by Carolrhoda Books, Inc.
Soft cover by First Avenue Editions
241 First Avenue North
Minneapolis, MN 55401

Library of Congress Cataloging-in-Publication Data

Liestman, Vicki.
  Columbus Day / by Vicki Liestman ; illustrations by Rick Hanson.
    p. cm. —(Carolrhoda on my own books)
  Summary: Relates the story of the discovery of America by
Christopher Columbus and gives the history of Columbus Day.
  ISBN 0-87614-444-X (lib. bdg.)
  ISBN 0-87614-559-4 (pbk.)
  1. Columbus Day—Juvenile literature. [1. Columbus Day.
2. Columbus, Christopher. 3. America—Discovery and exploration—
Spanish.] I. Hanson, Rick, ill. II. Title. III. Series:
Carolrhoda on my own book.
E120.L76   1991
970.01'5—dc20
                                          90-23663
                                              CIP
                                              AC

Manufactured in the United States of America

  2 3 4 5 6 7 8 9 10 00 99 98 97 96 95 94 93 92

Author's Note

Columbus Day is the holiday that commemorates the discovery of North and South America. But was it really Christopher Columbus who discovered these lands? More than 400 years before Columbus was even born, in about A.D. 1000, a Viking explorer named Leif Ericson landed on the coast of North America. Ericson tried to start a colony, but he and his men were driven away by the Native Americans who already lived there. So was it Leif Ericson who discovered North and South America? The word *discover* means to find out something that is unknown. But America wasn't unknown to the Native Americans.

The truth seems to be that America wasn't discovered at all, any more than Europe or Africa or Asia were discovered. So why is Christopher Columbus so important? Columbus's voyage established a lasting connection between Europe and North and South America. To some people, this connection meant exciting adventures and new opportunities. To others, it meant hardship and even death. But whether the results were good or bad, Christopher Columbus made a voyage that changed the world.

Five hundred years ago, the people who
lived in Europe were just beginning to learn
about the rest of the world.

Most Europeans knew the world was round.
But no one knew for sure just how big it was.

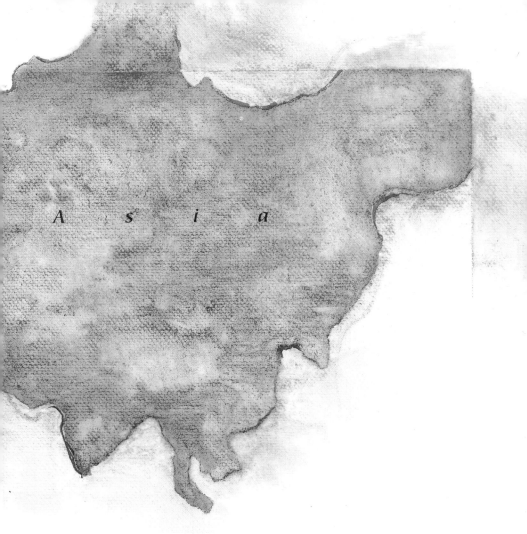

They knew that east of Europe was Asia.
They knew that south of Europe was Africa.
And they knew that west of Europe was a
big ocean.

Some people thought there might be
other lands across the ocean.
Others said this was nonsense.
But most Europeans were not thinking
about finding new lands.
They wanted to find a new way to get to
a place they already knew about.
This place was called the Indies.

The Indies were part of Asia.

China, India, Japan, and some islands
near China were all part of the Indies.

There was gold in the Indies.

There were jewels and spices, too.

Some Europeans wanted to go
to the Indies to buy these things.

They wanted to bring these goods back
to Europe and sell them.

But they could not get to the Indies.

People called Turks lived on the land
between Europe and the Indies.
The Turks would not let the Europeans
cross their land.
So the Europeans had to find
another way to get to the Indies.
If they could not get there by land,
maybe they could get there by sea.

One person who thought a lot about the
Indies was Christopher Columbus.
Columbus was a sailor.
He was born in the city of Genoa in 1451.
(Genoa is part of Italy now.)
By 1477, Columbus had moved to Lisbon,
in Portugal.
Lisbon is on the ocean.
So the city was full of sailors.
Columbus and the other sailors
talked about sailing to the Indies.
A ship would have to sail south around Africa
before sailing east to the Indies, they said.
This would be a long, hard voyage.

A few people were talking about another idea.
They knew the world was round.
So a ship should be able to get to the Indies
by sailing west instead of east.
Christopher Columbus liked this idea
so much he decided to try it himself.
Columbus knew that the voyage
would cost a lot of money.
He did not have a lot of money.
So in 1484, Columbus went to
King John II of Portugal.

He told the king
what he wanted to do.
Then he asked the king to pay for the voyage.
King John told Columbus that his idea
would not work.
He would not give Columbus any money.
Columbus did not give up.

In 1485, Columbus went to Spain.

He asked Queen Isabella and King Ferdinand

to pay for the voyage.

He told them he would bring the Christian

religion to the people of the Indies.

He told them he would bring back

great treasures.

But Spain was fighting a war.

The king and queen did not have any

extra money to give to Columbus.

Columbus still did not give up.

Seven years later, in 1492,
Spain won its war.
Queen Isabella and King Ferdinand decided
to send Columbus to look for the Indies.

It took months to get ready for the voyage.

First Columbus had to find some ships.

He found three ships.

They were called the *Santa María,*

the *Niña,* and the *Pinta.*

Next he had to find people to sail the ships.

This was not easy.

The trip would be dangerous.

No one knew how far they would have to sail.

No one knew what they would find on the way.

Columbus finally found
90 sailors to make the trip.
They loaded the ships with food.
There were biscuits and beans,
salted meat and fish.
They brought water and wine to drink.
On September 6, 1492, three very full ships
left Spain's Canary Islands for the Indies.

One night, the sailors saw
fire shooting across the sky.
It was probably just a meteor.
But the sailors said it was a sign
they would never come back.

For a while, the ocean was covered with weeds.
The sailors said the weeds
were a sign of danger.
Columbus said they were a sign of land.
They sailed on and on.
But they did not find land.

The sailors were afraid.

What if they ran out of food?

What if they ran out of water?

What if they sailed on and on forever?

They wanted to turn back.

But Columbus said they must keep going.

It was two o'clock in the morning
on October 12, 1492.
A sailor on the *Pinta*
looked out into the night.
He saw something white.
It was an island!
"Land, land!" he cried.
The sailors were happy
because the long trip was over.
Columbus was happy because he thought
he had found the Indies.

The sun came up.
Columbus and some other men
climbed into small boats.
They rowed to the island.
When they got out of their boats,
they saw some people.
The people were watching them.

Columbus made a speech.

He named the island San Salvador.

He said it belonged to

the queen and king of Spain.

Columbus thought he was in the Indies.
So he called the people Indians.
Of course, the people and the island
already had names.
The people were the Taino (TY-noh).
They called their island Guanahaní
(gwahn-ah-hahn-EE).
The Taino did not speak Spanish.
They did not know Columbus was
taking their island away from them.

The Taino gave the Spaniards
parrots and balls of cotton.
The Spaniards gave the Taino
bells and glass beads.
The Taino seemed to like the Spaniards.
They treated the Spaniards like friends.
Columbus liked the Taino, too.
But he did not think of them as friends.
He said he thought they would make
very good servants.

Columbus saw that some of the Taino
wore clothes, and some didn't.
He saw that some of them had painted
their faces bright colors.
And he saw that some of the Taino had
pieces of metal hanging from their noses.
And the metal was gold!
Columbus made signs with his hands
to ask where the gold was from.
The people pointed to the south.
That must be the way to
China and Japan and more gold!
When Columbus left the island,
he made some of the Taino go with him.
He wanted them to help him find gold.

For weeks, the Spaniards sailed
from island to island.
They saw other people besides the Taino.
(Columbus called them all Indians.)
But they did not find China or Japan.
And they did not find gold.
In December, they stopped at a big island.
Columbus named the island La Española
(LAH ehs-pah-NYOH-lah).
There they met more Indians.
The Spaniards liked these Indians.
They had gold.
They did not have very much gold.
But it was more gold than the Spaniards
had seen so far.
They decided to stay for a while.

On Christmas Day, the *Santa María*
had an accident.
It ran into some rocks in the harbor.
It started to sink.
The Indians helped the Spaniards.
They took everything off the ship
and brought it all to shore.
Then the ship sank.

Now Columbus had only two ships.

There were too many people for just two ships.

Columbus decided to leave

the extra sailors on the island.

He would come back for them later.

They built a fort for the sailors to live in.
They called it La Navidad
(LAH nah-vee-DAHD).
This means Christmas in Spanish.
Soon after that, Columbus sailed for home.
Columbus brought many things back to Spain
to show Queen Isabella and King Ferdinand.
He brought them gold, of course.
He brought them parrots and big rats.
He brought them dogs that never barked.
He brought them cotton and lizard skins.
And he brought them six young Indian men.
The queen and king were very happy.
They said Columbus was a hero.

A few months later, Columbus went back
to La Española.
Something awful had happened.
La Navidad had been burned down.
All of the people who lived there were dead.

Columbus went to the Indians
who had helped him before.
He asked them what had happened.
They told him that the Spaniards
had done awful things to some of
the other Indians on the island.
So those Indians had killed the Spaniards.
After that, things got worse and worse.

Columbus kept sailing from island to island.
He had promised to send the queen
and king great treasures.
He had to find more gold.
But he could not find enough gold.
He looked for something else to send.
All around him were Indians.
He decided to send Indians instead of gold.
Columbus loaded five hundred people
onto ships.
He took them away from their homes.
He took them away from their
families.
He sent them to Spain.

The Indians who were left behind
were not any luckier.
The Spaniards made them slaves, too.
Then the Spaniards killed many of the slaves.

The Spaniards killed some of the slaves
because they could not do the work.
And they killed some of them
for no reason at all.

Some of the Spaniards who lived on the
islands changed their minds about
Christopher Columbus.
They didn't think he was a hero anymore.
But it was not because of the way
the Indians were treated.
Most of the Spaniards didn't care
about that at all.
They were not happy with their new lives.
They blamed Columbus.
They said he was a bad leader.

Columbus died in 1506.
He never knew he had not found
a new way to get to the Indies.
He never knew he had found
much more than that.

The years went by.
More and more Europeans
sailed across the ocean.
They wanted to see the lands on the other side.
They found there was much more land
than Columbus had known about.
And there were many more people
than Columbus had seen.
The Europeans called the lands
on the other side of the ocean
North America and South America.

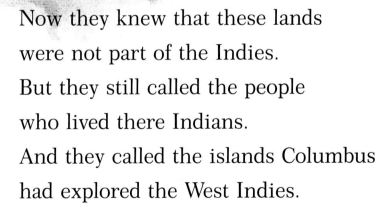

America

West
Indies

Now they knew that these lands
were not part of the Indies.
But they still called the people
who lived there Indians.
And they called the islands Columbus
had explored the West Indies.

45

Still more years went by.

Some people changed their minds about
Christopher Columbus again.

He had found a new land, they said.

He must have been very brave
and smart, they said.

He must have been a hero.

On October 12, 1892, it had been exactly
four hundred years since Columbus
first came to America.

The people of the United States
wanted to celebrate this important day.

They had already named schools
after Columbus.

They had already named cities
after Columbus.

But they wanted to do more.

COLUMBUS AVE.

D.C.

**COLUMBUS
ELEMENTAR**

**COLUMBIA
COLLEGE**

COLUMBUS
OHIO

President Benjamin Harrison made
October 12, 1892, Columbus Day.
People celebrated all over
the United States that day.
The biggest celebration was in New York City.
It lasted for five days.

There were flags and streamers
everywhere.
There were parades almost every day.
There was even a boat parade on the river.
To remember the day, New Yorkers put
up a statue of Christopher Columbus.
Some people liked celebrating
Columbus Day so much that they
wanted to do it every year.

In 1937, President Franklin Roosevelt
made Columbus Day a holiday to be
celebrated every year on October 12.
People celebrate Columbus Day in many ways.
Some people do not have to work that day.
Many cities have Columbus Day parades.
In schools, children learn about
the famous voyage.
The day is also remembered in
Canada, Mexico, Spain, and Italy.
Many countries in South America and
Central America celebrate it, too.

Every year, we remember the good things
about Columbus and his exciting voyage.
But there is something many people forget.
We forget about the people
Columbus called Indians.
(Indians are called Native Americans now.)
We forget about the awful way
the Native Americans were treated.
We forget about the people who died.
Maybe it's time to think of
Columbus Day in a new way.
October 12 can be a day to tell the whole story
of the voyage that changed the world.
It can be a day to remember
the Native Americans.
And it can be a day to remember that when
we explore, we must be good to the life
we meet along the way.

It has been five hundred years since
Columbus made his famous voyage.
Explorers have been all over the world.
They have been to the bottom of the sea.
They have been to the tops of mountains.
But now there is a new place to explore.
People are just beginning to learn
about outer space.

We know that it is very big.
But no one knows for sure *how* big it is.
We know that there are planets,
like Mercury and Jupiter.
Explorers called astronauts are flying in
spaceships farther and farther into space.

Who will be the one to find
lands that are new to us?
Who will be the one to find other beings?
Maybe it will be you.
If it is, how will you treat those beings?
Maybe you can think about it
on Columbus Day.